First Publishe

JD Wildi Publis

Text copyright © DebbieWildi

E-mail: debbie@truerelax.co.uk

www.truerelax.co.uk

ISBN 978-0-9568513-2-1

Printed in the UK by

Lightning Source UK Ltd.

Registered in England and Wales

Company number 4042196

Registered office 5 New Street Square, London, EC4A 3TW

This book is dedicated to every fabulous teenager out there in this wonderful world (yes, even the grumpy ones) and especially my very own fabulous teen too.

Contents

Introduction — Page 1

Chapter 1 : Confidence – or, how to feel like the uber cool kid in the playground — Page 3

Chapter 2 : Anger Management – or, controlling the beast within — Page 16

Chapter 3 : Self Harm – or, how to safely take away the inner angst — Page 27

Chapter 4 : Sleep Solvers – or, how to get your ZZZ time! — Page 33

Chapter 5 : Panic attacks – or, how to beat the freaky fright monster in your mind — Page 44

Chapter 6 : Bring on the depression – or, avoiding the sure fire triggers that will guarantee a glum day — Page 51

Chapter 7 : Mood Lifters – or, how to get happy — Page 76

Chapter 8 : The Life Plan – or, how to get direction — Page 78

Chapter 9 : Bullying – or, how to beat it, be assertive, and get your groove back! — Page 81

Useful Links — Page 91

Introduction

Life for a Teen can be tough with a capital T.

I cringe as I remember the feeling of dread, as I would walk around the corner at school and see the 'cool kids', or that boy i fancied but couldn't ever speak to without stuttering and turning bright pink.

Then there was the time I actually joined the 'cool kids'. I became one of the 'in' crowd; running around getting into trouble, ditching school, preferring to smoke and drink just to try and fit in.

However, to be honest that was *just* as stressful as being one of the 'divvies'; always trying to keep up the pretence that I was tough, and in order to be 'cool' I had to join in as they laughed at the 'school drip' and called them names.
This is what I call 'compromising my values', in other words, It felt wrong. So I stopped.
Instead I stuck up for the 'drippy kid' and got in more and more fights with the 'cool kids', which meant more and more fights with the teachers. School turned into one big political minefield. If you weren't cool then you didn't fit in, if you *were* cool then you had to keep it up Phew, it's exhausting!

All this, and we haven't even reached the subject of homework yet; or exam stress, or early morning starts, or late night studying, or feeling dumb when the rest of the class understands something that you don't, or the disagreements with Mum and Dad, or the introduction of a Step-parent, or Step siblings.

Do I have the best shoes? Why are my friends leaving me out? Am I too fat? Am I too thin? Too short? Too tall? Will I ever get a boyfriend/girlfriend? Will I ever stop feeling so tired? I just want to SLEEEEEP!!!
And I haven't even mentioned the dreaded H word, yes...

HORMONES!

See, it's tough. Not all the time; but for enough of it.

One day it will pass. In future years you may even say words of wisdom to your own Teen such as *"you don't know how good you've got it"* and *"Schooldays are the best days of your life"* blah blah blah.

However, you *do* have to be a teen for a while longer, so until then, you have me with you...Well, this book anyway; to help guide you through the tough bits, and laugh with you at the fun bits. Because it isn't all doom and gloom. It can actually be great fun, and it honestly can become the best time in your life.

Chapter.1. Confidence- or

how to feel like the uber cool kid in the playground

Confidence! Now that's a

powerful word.

Great if you're lucky enough to have bags of it. However, for some reason it often seems in short supply during our teenage years.

Do you feel confident when you walk along the road?

Do you think you look good?

Do you feel comfortable asking the teacher a question in front of the rest of the class, or do you keep your hand down and fail to ask the question for fear of being sniggered at? …

And, what if you *do* ask the question in class, will

your classmates think you are a geek for being interested in the subject?

You may ask yourself…

"Are my legs too fat?"

"Is my hair too frizzy for that hairstyle?"

"Are my biceps too small?"

"Am I too spotty?"

The simple and honest answer to these questions above is *"NO!"*

Who decides whether your legs are too fat? Too fat for whom?

Only you and your Doctor can decide if you are comfortable and healthy being the weight you are at.

And here is an extremely important secret...most of your fellow pupils will breathe a HUGE sigh of relief if you put up your hand to ask a question, because secretly most of the class were probably hoping that someone would, so that they didn't have to put up their hand and ask it.

You will actually have helped out the whole class. They will now understand the subject because you asked the teacher to explain it in more detail.

Secretly you have become the class hero, not the class geek!

Here is the thing... we worry too much. In fact we spend so much time worrying about the things that we may be 'bad' at, that we do not notice the things that we actually *are* good at. So here is a confidence boosting exercise, and trust me, it works….

Confidence boosting

Try it task!

Write down <u>3</u> things that you know you are good at. This could be anything from being a good friend, making people laugh, to being a good dancer. Anything at all.

Go on, do it now, don't be embarrassed or shy. It's only me and you here. Go on. If you don't want to write it here put it on a separate piece of paper, but keep it somewhere safe so that if you are having an unconfident day you can look at it and bring that confidence back…

"I am good at…"

Picture it, feel it, be it!

Visualisation may be words you have heard before, if it isn't then allow me to explain....

To 'visualise' something means to picture it in your mind. Use your imagination and you can see anything with your eyes closed. Just like daydreaming.

The good news here is that the younger you are, the easier it normally is to visualise something. It's usually only us old and cynical wrinklies that find it harder. Don't ask me why, I haven't a clue, I just know that when I teach visualisation exercises to children and teens they can do it, they LOVE it and find it easy to let their imaginations run free.

However, if you do find it tricky, then let me give you a word of advice - this *does* get easier with practise and if at first you find it difficult to picture things behind your closed eyes, then keep at it. I promise it works.

But, how do they work?

We have two parts to our mind – our 'subconscious' (sometimes also called 'unconscious mind'), and our 'conscious mind'.

The subconscious mind holds all of our beliefs and fears. For example, if we believe that spiders are scary, that information is stored here.

We can talk to our 'conscious mind' (the part that we use to think with) and tell it that *"Spiders are not frightening"* but it is our subconscious mind that we need to tell. This is the bit that stores the info. I suppose you could say this is our 'hard drive'.

Subconscious - Stores our info

The subconscious mind is also the part that holds our beliefs about ourselves; For example, if we have ever been told that we are *'useless'*, or *'ugly'*, or *'fat'* then this information can become stored in our subconscious. So we need to delete it because it is rubbish information. It isn't true.

This is where the visualisations come in. You can only really talk to your subconscious mind when you are relaxed. It doesn't really listen properly otherwise.

So first we relax, then do a simple visualisation to tell our subconscious mind that we are great. And it listens. **Simple!**

So here follows some easy peasy visualisation exercises. They will boost your confidence and raise your self-esteem, meaning that if you don't think too much of yourself right now, then you will after doing these.

Some of the most successful people in the world believe that the more you picture yourself achieving what you want; the more likely you are to get it.

Many scientists are now backing up this claim by proving that the more positive our thoughts are, the more likely we are to have a happy and successful life.

We get what we think about! *'Energy flows where focus goes'* (in other words if we focus on bad things and expect the worst to happen, then more often than not, it will) If this is true then it makes sense to do the opposite. Let's focus on the good things that we want, not the bad.

Positive thoughts = happy humans

BUT HOW DO WE READ THE VISUALISATIONS WHEN WE ARE RELAXING WITH OUR EYES CLOSED?

Well, you can either nip to the shops and buy yourself some very expensive, and extremely magical glasses that enable you to read through closed eyes (and don't actually exist), or, more realistically you can ask a good friend or parent to read it to you - maybe take it in turns to read it to each other,

Or, the most popular way, is to read it through by yourself a couple of times, then close your eyes and just visualise the parts that you remember. (Don't worry if you can't remember all of the visualisation As long as you can remember some of it that's fine). The more that you read it through and practise it, the more of it you will remember.

Do these exercises and you will soon start to see what we can all see...that you are truly **awesome!**

So let's get started, there 's no time to lose, you're getting older, wrinklier and more cynical by the second (joke!)...

Confidence Boosting Visualisations

Visualisation 1.

WIN AND SUCCEED

Find a comfortable place to sit or lie down and close your eyes….

Take some long, slow deep breaths to relax you.

When you feel calm, think about something that you would like to be successful at. Now this can be anything…winning a race, or a singing or dancing competition, or climbing the highest mountain, or surfing the highest wave

(Do not limit it, this can be the biggest best achievement ever, it's not important whether it is realistic at the moment or not. The important thing is the good feeling that this visualisation will give you)

Really go for it! The sky is the limit. Your daydream today can be whatever you wish it to

Start:

In your mind, see yourself doing the winning achievement, whatever you wish it to be.

Really use your imagination, think about how you would feel whilst you do it. Maybe you feel afraid and nervous? Or even excited?

(A really good tip to help your visualisation feel real is to use all of your 5 senses – sound, sight, touch, smell, taste)

By this I mean imagine what you would be able to hear in your daydream, the crowds cheering you on? Or the roar of the sea whilst you surf the highest wave?

Would there be any kind of smell? For example, maybe if you were climbing the highest mountain you could smell the fresh air or grass?

What would the microphone feel like in your hand when you are belting your lungs out singing your winning song? Or how would your body feel as you dance your heart out?

Now, just enjoy the feeling. Notice how it feels as people pat you on the back and say well done, smile and revel in your success. Open your eyes when you feel ready.

Visualisation 2.

RECOGNISE YOUR AWESOMENESS!

Close your eyes and take a moment to think about something special that you have done for someone.

Now, this can be anything from smiling at a stranger to making a cup of tea for someone.

Just think about how much you will have helped them. How happy you would have made them. The little old lady who lives alone would have been over the moon to see your smile I bet, and the happiness your busy parent/carer/grandparent might feel at putting their feet up and having a warm cuppa made for them will be huge.

If you think back, you will remember a time when you made someone's day. No matter how small it will seem to you, it probably meant a lot to that person.

Have a think, go on…

Then, smile, and congratulate yourself on the fact that you are a great human being, and recognise just how great you can be…

Celebrate your awesomeness!

You are …

Visualisation 3.

OVERCOME YOUR FEAR

Are you afraid of anything? Spiders? Moths? The dark? Small spaces? Bullies? Exams? Being alone?

Fear is a part of our lives, but it doesn't have to be.

This visualisation will help you conquer your fears.

By imagining yourself doing the very thing that you are afraid of, you can help yourself to overcome these fears, because you then realise it's not so bad.

Start:

Use your imagination and see yourself confronting your fear. Start off very slowly. For example imagine yourself walking up to the spider, or into a dark room, or imagine yourself alone, sitting an exam, or facing the bully.

Remember that you are safe, and no harm will come to you at all.

How do you feel? Nervous? Fearful? That's ok, these are normal emotions.

Breathe deeply and calmly and know that you are safe. Keep picturing the scene.

Now see yourself actually enjoying it. Visualise yourself smiling, looking and feeling confident. How great do you feel now? Knowing you have done the thing you have always been frightened of. It's a great feeling isn't it?

The more that you do this exercise the less you will be afraid. By visualising the scene you will see that it's not really that bad, and that your fears can be overcome.

Studies show that if we 'see' ourselves overcoming our fear, and feel positive about it, then it will actually become easier to do in real life.

You can do…

ANYTHING!

CHAPTER .2. ANGER MANAGEMENT – or
controlling the beast within

What makes you angry? Just take a moment to think about what really makes your blood boil. What is the little demon that makes you wanna

SCRREEEEEAAM?

If you just spend a few moments thinking about what it is that regularly makes you cross then you can be prepared for it when it comes.

When that demon rears its' head you will be ready to tackle it head on with a **BIG,**

ANGRY... **giggle.**

Yes that's right, I said giggle.

WHAT???

What do you mean, giggle?

Well exactly that... when faced with a moment that would normally make you want to shout, just try a giggle instead.

Easier said than done right?

Wrong!

If the anger is justified (in other words, if there is a very good reason to feel angry) then it will be fairly hard to control it without practice, however most times anger isn't really about the situation in front of you, it can be caused by raging hormones building up in your system, or tiredness (which is quite often the number one culprit) and often when you look at it, there is no need to feel angry. It's just a feeling that has overtaken you and got you in a strong, massive headlock.

So how do you get out of that grip of anger? How do you free yourself from it?

Laugh at your anger gremlin when you feel it coming.

When you feel that rise of rage in the pit of your stomach caused by something that would normally make you feel slightly irritable. STOP and THINK. *"Is this really justified, or is it my silly gremlin again".*

For example: if the anger is caused by your little brother or sister moving your hairbrush, then yes, I can see that's completely annoying, however does it really justify a big screaming shout down?

Maybe you can laugh at your gremlin instead and refuse to give in to it, and do one of the anger busting techniques featured over the next few pages.

Then have a word with your brother/sister or parent/carer and explain how frustrating it is. Believe me no one listens when someone is shouting at them…

FACT! When you explain tin a calm way to a person

just how you are feeling, they are much more likely to listen. It's true, try it, it works, not always, but the majority of the time. Worth a try eh?

ANGER BUSTING TECHNIQUES

When we feel like we're going to explode with rage, it helps if we have a place to vent that anger (somewhere to get rid of it safely). This is why I included these techniques in this chapter. They are simple exercises that will take away the rage at that crucial moment when you are not quite sure what to do with it. Here follows a few of my tried and tested favourites that have proved so popular with teens in my classes….

Technique1: STRESS BLOW

This is like screaming, but without the sound. Wouldn't it feel great to scream at the top of our voices when we feel anger rising? However, it isn't a real option. Unfortunately we can't go around shouting and screaming as it upsets others and makes us look like fools. So this is the next best alternative…

When you feel the ARRRRGHHH ready to escape your mouth, take in a really deep breath, and….

BLOOOOOOWWWW!

Blow the air out of your body really hard.

Do it again…

And again…

How do you feel now?

As well as getting rid of that tension in your body it tires you out, therefore slowing down the adrenaline that's rushing around your body making you hopping mad.

Problem solved!

Technique 2: FLOOR DRUMMING

Now this may look slightly crazy so it may be best to take yourself somewhere private, such as your bedroom, or somewhere private at school (if you are at school when the anger takes over)…

Start by taking a deep breath.

Now as you breathe out, drum the palms of your hands on the floor, or bed, or even a wall.(Do not punch as this will hurt your hand, maybe damage the wall/floor, and may get you into trouble)

Drum faster and faster until you feel more relaxed, and the angry moment has passed - or at least calmed down a notch or two.

Now just breathe deeply and slowly and feel yourself relax completely.

Technique 3: PILLOW POUNDING

This is a great one, which always results in lots of giggles when we do it in my classes. It takes all of that anger and lets it out in a safe way…

Pick up your pillow by holding two corners and literally beat your bed with it. Lift it way over your head then bring it down – thump! On your bed. It won't break anything, or harm anyone.

It feels great and you use so much energy doing it, so it's also a fun workout. Result, eh!

Stress zapping techniques

These techniques are another fabulous way to throw away anger, and in fact any yucky feelings that you may be experiencing. They can take away worries and stress in a simple and enjoyable way…

Exercise 1: Cleansing shower

This is a lovely exercise which really leaves you feeling stress free and happy…

The next time you are in the shower or bath, imagine you are washing away your stress. As you cleanse your body, tell yourself that you are rinsing your worries and negative (upsetting) feelings away.

You can actually do this at any time, you do not need to be in the bath or shower. Just take yourself off to a private place and go through the action of wiping your body down.

By this I mean that you do a sweeping action with your hands down your arms, then down your legs as if you are sweeping away dust from your clothes. Tell yourself that you are wiping away the stress and negativity. (You can even do this one in front of your mates if you need to. It simply looks as though you are wiping something off your clothes…no odd looks heading your way)

This exercise works by using the power of your mind. If you tell yourself that you wish to wash away the negativity, then you are instructing your mind to do so.

If you tell it often enough, believe me, it will begin to listen to you!

Exercise 2: Let Rip!

No, this is not an exercise in breaking wind, it is actually a fantastic way of letting go of something that's really bothering you…..

If something is making you really angry or sad, then write it down. Either write a letter to the person making you sad (you are not going to send the letter, but just writing down how you feel can really help take those yucky thoughts and feelings out of your mind where they are being stored and doing you and your health no good at all)

So start by writing this line **'I am angry because….**

Or

'I am sad because….

Then just let the words flow. (Now remember no one will see this so really get your anger out, really let your sadness flow, even have a little cry if you feel like it....even, dare I say it? – use bad words. No one will know).

Now here comes the good bit...

When you have finished; read it, and decide that you want to let go of those feelings, you do not need them, they are making you feel rubbish.

So on the count of 3 rip the letter to little pieces, teeny tiny bits, and as you rip, feel good and laugh and know that you are in control of how you feel.

Now throw it in the bin. Right at the bottom. And **SMILE!**

Chapter 3 Self Harm – or how to safely take away the inner angst

This is such a controversial subject, and I had to think long and hard about whether to include this section in the book or not. But the more that people do NOT talk about 'taboo' subjects (this means subjects that are kept hidden), the more the sufferers often suffer alone.

So let's talk about it, not shy away from it.

Let us stand up and be proud enough to say that we all get stressed sometimes. We all sometimes reach that point of snapping, that is nothing to be ashamed of, but it is HOW we choose to deal with those feelings that is the key.

I used to self-harm when I was a teen and if I had known more about it back then (in the olden days) then I would have found ways to stop sooner than I did. However, it was not talked about in schools, or books, or anywhere. No one understood it, and certainly no one tackled the very shocking subject. So let's be the brave ones shall we. And tackle it together.

Let's choose to let out these destructive feelings in a healthy way. We still need to let the feelings out because bottling things up inside only causes more stress…. but let's get them out in an effective and safe way.

So here goes…

When I was in my teens I saw a fantastic counsellor who taught me <u>two</u> great techniques. They are basically about taking those feelings of frustration and letting them out safely.

Self-harming can be described as a release. When those bottled up feelings are about to explode and we don't know what to do with them, people who self-harm can be inclined to grab a sharp object and scrape or cut themselves with it, which can bring a feeling of release.

(Although I absolutely MUST add that this feeling of release does not last, and you ALWAYS end up feeling worse afterward).

Every day recognise something great about yourself. No matter how small. You are unique and clever (sometimes that cleverness is in something other than school work. It does not matter EVERYONE is clever at something).

Now the key is to start treating yourself as you would your best friend. You certainly wouldn't attack your friend with a pair of scissors would you? You wouldn't call your friend nasty names and hurt them. So please don't do it to yourself.

I don't even know you, but I know that you are fabulous.

Why?

Because everyone has fabulous qualities about them. You just need to look for them sometimes to recognise what they are.

Don't you think that if you are feeling sad, frustrated or angry you deserve a cuddle, not a cut? Give yourself a cuddle, be kind to yourself.

However, this is sometimes easier than done, especially if you have already developed the awful habit of self-harm. So in the meantime whilst you are learning to recognise how wonderful you are I want to show you the two techniques that I used as a teenager- until I realised just how amazing I am also, and started to treat myself with the love and care that I truly deserve.

Technique 1: Arm Scribbling

Sounds bonkers doesn't it?

But trust me, it works.

Keep a pen handy, probably in your bedroom drawer or somewhere handy.

When you feel that angst coming and you feel the urge to self-harm, grab the pen.

Now scribble all over your arm. You will notice that you are still venting your anger. You may be scribbling fairly hard, BUT the key point here is that you will not damage yourself.

In time, you will scribble more and more softly, and less and less, until you do not feel the need to do it anymore. The addiction of self-harming can be broken, and this is a great way to wean yourself from it.

Technique 2: Icebreaker

This technique helps you to vent your feelings in a safe way and is extremely effective…

Instead of reaching for a sharp implement, take an ice cube. Now squeeze it in your hand really hard.

Feel the cold, it becomes colder and colder, and almost feels quite painful after a while.

However, it will not damage you, so it's a safer way to 'self harm' Does that makes sense?

By concentrating on the feeling of the cold ice in your hand, you will often find that your focus is taken away from your problem and you will then feel more relaxed and calm again.

Breathe deeply, wait for the feelings to pass and throw the ice away when you feel ready.

PARENTAL /CARER MESSAGE: Obviously, it would be ideal not to need these techniques in the first place and some people reading this may even think me totally irresponsible for suggesting them. However, I have seen them work. They can wean the sufferer from self -

harming, then as they use the other techniques in this book, they will hopefully find the negative feelings that trigger this behaviour will disappear altogether, but in the meantime let's keep them safe by suggesting these safer alternative solutions.

Chapter .4. Sleep Solvers – or how to get your ZZZ time!

When we mammals are not getting enough sleep everything feels ten times harder doesn't it?

Our brains find it so difficult to concentrate, and a simple task can turn into a mammoth one.

We lose our focus, making schoolwork harder, and emotions run high. We can become irritable and turn into the most ultimate grump monster overnight!

So we need to tackle it…

When we can't sleep, this is called this insomnia. This can happen for all sorts of reasons; eating too close to bedtime, drinking caffeine based drinks, and, of course, stress!

The techniques that feature on the next few pages are designed to help you beat insomnia, and banish those sleepless nights.

Hey, it's time to get your sparkly eyes back…

The 3B Method

I had been teaching a stress busting technique called the *3B Method to* adults suffering with insomnia, or anger, for long while, when suddenly more and more teenagers started coming along to the sessions, either along with their parents, or on their own.

I soon realised that insomnia (and anger) was becoming a big problem for teens in our society today, so I therefore set up *Teen relax* sessions.

The *3B Method* used in this book has been used by a variety of teenagers aged between 11 and 18 years, and the results really do speak for themselves.

The *3B method* is a fantastic tool to help you get to sleep at night. Now I will teach you how to use it too…

HOW DOES THE 3B METHOD WORK?

If you help your body to relax by doing the body and breathing exercise, then your brain will start to unwind and get ready for sleep – and if it doesn't, then zap it with the *Paper Method (see page 39).*

First do step 1

Followed straight away by step 2

Then step 3 if you need it

__STEP 1:__ **Relax your breathing**

As you breathe in, count slowly in your mind to 3 at the same time. Make your in-breath last for the whole count. 1- 2- 3.

As you breathe out do the same. Make your out-breath last for the count of 3.

Repeat this nice and slowly. Breathe in for the count of 3, and then out for the count of 3. Long, slow, deep breaths.

STEP 2: Relax your body

Find a comfortable position, if this is possible. (However, this exercise can be carried out anywhere; standing in the bus queue for example, or a school classroom as this exercise is also a great tool for helping beat exam nerves), If you are using it to help you get to sleep – then get yourself comfortable in bed...

And just follow the simple steps by relaxing all the parts of your body, from your head down to your toes ...

Relax your jaw, don't clench it.

Relax your neck.

Physically relax your shoulders. Drop them down.

Breathe in deeply, and then breathe out slowly to relax your chest.

Next relax your stomach muscles.

Relax your legs, feel your thigh and calf muscles. Let go of tension held in your leg muscles.

Finally, relax your ankles and feet.

Now just continue to breathe in and out slowly and deeply,

STEP 3: The Paper Method

You may feel completely relaxed just by doing the first 2 steps (relaxing your breathing and body), but if your thoughts keep racing around inside your head, or you find you are worrying about something and are finding it difficult to relax, you can use the *paper method…*

> *If you notice that your mind has wandered and you are thinking about something else, or keep worrying about something in particular simply picture a piece of paper in your mind.*
>
> *This piece of paper represents your thought/worry.*
>
> *Now imagine that you are screwing up the piece of paper and throwing it away.*
>
> *And take your focus back to your slow deep breathing (breathe in for the count of 3, and out for the count of 3)*
>
> *Every time that you notice a thought or worry is popping into your head, just keep throwing those pieces of paper away. Throw your thoughts away and focus on your calm breathing.*

The more that you practice the *3B method*, the more relaxed you will become. It will take away feelings of stress, and is especially great for helping you overcome anxiety and panic attacks.

It is perfect to use before, or even during exams. And, of course, for those moments when you cannot sleep and you want to.

It only take minutes, or even seconds to do, and once you get used to doing it you can do it anywhere at all to help to calm yourself whenever you want to.

Once you practice the *Paper method* you can use it to throw any unwanted thought out of your head. Banish negative, yucky, worries, leaving heaps of space in there for nice thoughts instead.

Winding down

It's so tempting to play game consoles, or chat on the Internet until you can hardly keep your eyes open isn't it?

However, these aren't great ways to help you 'wind down'. By winding down I mean getting your body and your mind ready for sleep.

When we are playing games, surfing the net, or chatting to friends our brains are active, they are working frantically hard, even though it might not feel like it at the time.

Our bodies are not getting ready for sleep (in other words, our muscles are not relaxing) because we aren't telling them to.

An un-relaxed body and mind will not just shut down and go to sleep because we expect it to. It needs to be told that its sleep time. So here are the various ways to tell them ….

1. **Relax your body by having a bath or shower.** This really is a wonderful way to unwind those muscles. Soak up the warmth and I am sure your body will soon get the message that this is lovely, soothing 'ahhhhh, relaxing time'.

2. **Do the 3B Method** (see page 35)

3. **Put on some relaxing music** OK so it's not the kind of music you want your mates to know exists on your MP3 player, but it really is worth downloading some relaxation music if you can. If not, you can buy it from any number of music shops, or online. Simply type 'relaxation music', or 'meditation music' into a search engine. Or download a relaxation 'app'. It is proven to slow down your heart rate, your breathing, and unwind your mind. You never know, you may enjoy it, I bet it surprises you!

4. **Peace and Quiet** It may seem obvious, however when I was a teenager I used to have the television in my bedroom turned up so loudly it was no wonder I didn't drop off to sleep. I used to turn on the TV at bedtime because I believed it 'helped' me sleep. It didn't. Once I realised that the sounds were keeping

me awake. I used to have it on with the sound down. The flickering lights of the television in the darkened room actually were relaxing, but the sound wasn't.

5. **No flickering lights.** Contrary to what I said above, many people cannot sleep with the constant flickering of lights, or, in fact, any lights in their place of sleep. Play around and see what works for you. Lamp on, lamp off? Nightlights? Or complete darkness. We are all different. See which helps you settle the most.

6. **Lavender** ahhh the beautiful aroma of relaxing lavender oil. This is renowned for helping us sleep. Use 5 drops in your bath, or simply place 2 drops on your pillow. (Use pure lavender 'essential', or 'aromatherapy' oil. Available from any chemist)

7. **Reading** A great way to unwind.

Chapter. 5. Panic Attacks – or how to beat the freaky fright monster in your mind

What is a panic attack?

A fast, racing heartbeat, butterflies in your stomach, sweaty palms, or sometimes simply a feeling of total fear, or dread.

Panic attacks can happen for no reason; they can come suddenly and unexpectedly. Sometimes we know the reason why: for example if you dislike crowded places and notice that you feel all of the symptoms above, then you can look after your well-being by choosing to stay away from crowded places, or going with people that you trust and feel comfortable with.

However, sometimes we have absolutely no idea why a panic attack starts.

When I used to suffer with them sometimes I could be walking along happily, or sitting watching television, when suddenly I would feel dread, as though I was really nervous, my heart would begin to pump faster and I would tremble.

At first I didn't have a clue what to do about it. I would just sit there and panic about the panic, causing even more panic. Until, before I knew it, I was full to the brim with panic. Panic, panic, panic, panic, panic, panic

ARRRGHHHHH!!!

Until… I learnt how to control them.

How did I do that?

I realised that by slowing down my breathing I could stop the feeling. It's simple, here's how…

Long, Slow, Deep breaths > Slow our heart rate

Long, Slow, Deep breaths > Create clearer thinking

Panic attacks are frightening. However, if we know that we **CAN** control them, then we **CAN** continue to do the things that normally bring on the attack. We **CAN** enter crowded places, because we are armed with the weapon to protect ourselves against the panic attack, should it rear its' ugly head.

Long, Slow, Deep breaths = our weapon against panic attacks.

And the best part is that our breath is always with us, we can't accidentally leave it at home. We don't need to pay for it. It's simply here, with us, always. So let's use it!

Long, Slow, Deep breaths will relax us whenever and wherever we are!

Fight or Flight

Sometimes a panic attack can begin simply because our body is tense. When our muscles are full of tension our mind is tense too. The reason for this is called *'Fight or Flight'*.

You may have heard of this before. It means that our body is getting ready to either fight or flee. Allow me to explain…

When we feel stressed our body takes this as a sign that we are about to be attacked (this stems from prehistoric times when the only problems that we ever had to stress about were big beasts coming to trample our homes, steal our food or gobble us up) So our body reacted by tensing our muscles to make them hard and strong allowing us to either fight the beast, or to use our strong muscles to run and 'flee' from it.

Our tense muscles would send a message to our brain telling it that there is a reason to be frightened.

Unfortunately the same still applies today, even though there is no scary beast to fight (well not often let's hope) - when we get stressed our muscles tense up, ready to 'fight' or take 'flight' from the beast.

So you see, when our muscles are tense our mind thinks, *"Uh-oh, tense muscles, there must be a reason to worry"*

Then before you know it your mind is stressed.

Put simply…

STRESS IN THE MIND > TENSE MUSCLES

TENSE MUSCLES > STRESS IN THE MIND

What should we do when fight or flight symptoms occur?

Use the *3B Method* featured in the insomnia chapter (page 35). As you know, the *3B Method* will relax your Breathing, your Body, and calm your Brain

By slowing our breathing we slow our heart rate. So let's use step.1 of the *3B* to relax our breathing.

We also want to relax our muscles right? So lets use step.2 of the *3B* to do this…

Then naturally our Brain will feel calmer and de-stressed, but if it still does not, then use step.3 *(The paper method)* to empty it of worrying or annoying thoughts.

The *3B Method* is perfect for combating panic attacks. Once you know how to relax your breathing, your body and calm your brain, panic attacks DON"T stand a chance.

Your Ultimate Weapon of choice? Yes you've guessed it…

The 3B Method

Hit the panic attack where it hurts, and show it who is boss.

Who is the boss of your feelings by the way?

You are!

Put simply…

3B Method = Bye Bye Panic Attack!

The most important point to remember is that panic attacks **can** be overcome. They are simply a physical reaction to stress, or muscle tension, and you **can** control them.

Remember **you** are the boss of your feelings!

Chapter. 6. Bring on the depression! - Or avoiding the sure fire triggers that will guarantee a glum day.

The reason this chapter is called 'Bring on the depression' rather than 'Beating depression, is because I want to spend time in this chapter looking at common things that trigger depression, and **how to avoid them.**

Sometimes depression happens due to hormonal changes in our bodies and these are unavoidable. This is where medication comes in handy ie: antidepressant pills.

But as we want to do all we can to avoid 'Bringing on the depression' we are going to look at some of the factors that can lead to it, and ways to make sure that you stay well away from them…

Cannabis

I can't express my views on this subject enough. I have seen so many friends go down the cannabis route, and then regret it. Because it's fun right?

WRONG!

The links between Cannabis and mental health issues cannot be ignored. There are way too many of them.

"Oh, but it's herbal, and how can anything that is herbal possibly be bad for us right?"

WRONG!

For a start to make a joint, the cannabis is mixed with tobacco, so there is obvious fact number one. It is NOT 'unharmful'.

However. The most terrifying fact that I want to point out to you is that there is a HUGE connection between cannabis and Schizophrenia (a horrendous mental illness, that has been likened to being stuck in a permanent bad dream – google 'Schizophrenia' – that should be enough to put you off the evil weed for life!)

It is well known now that cannabis **can** trigger Schizophrenia, and Psychosis (imagining things that aren't there/paranoia)

Some health professionals believe that even as little as *one* joint has been known to trigger it. Seriously!

Some people can cope seemingly well for years just enjoying the odd spliff. Then suddenly out of 'nowhere' comes anxiety, panic attacks, depression, even suicidal thoughts or hearing voices. If this herb can trigger these disorders then is it really so 'unharmful'?

Unfortunately I have seen it first-hand many times. I have seen friends change from fun loving, intelligent, creative, party people, into tired, depressed, anxious, extremely paranoid adults with no motivation or love for life.

Let's look at this last fact - **Lack of motivation**. This is no coincidence. Cannabis makes our brains fuzzy; this is half the fun; a crazy, confused feeling that makes us giggle.

However, this fuzzy feeling continues in our brains, even when the high has worn off. Our brains can't work properly in the sludge that cannabis causes. Thinking becomes harder, which causes frustration. Tiredness sets in and we become so unmotivated. We just can't be bothered.

How do you see yourself in your future? Happy, healthy, successful, wealthy? Living an exciting and challenging life? Having the freedom to buy what you want, when you want? Going on sunny holidays? Seeing the world? Wearing fabulous clothes? Going to great concerts and festivals? Having enough money to go out with friends to fun places?

OR living with next to no money because you can't hold down a job? Coughing, aching, and with a head full of anxiety and depression. OR even worse – in hospital with mental health problems.

Think about it, and you decide, because **your** future is in **your** hands. Help yourself avoid depression by staying away from the boring stoned crowd, and sticking with the fun loving, successful ones.

Alcohol/ Ecstasy /Cocaine/ Ketamine (K)/ Amphetamine (speed)

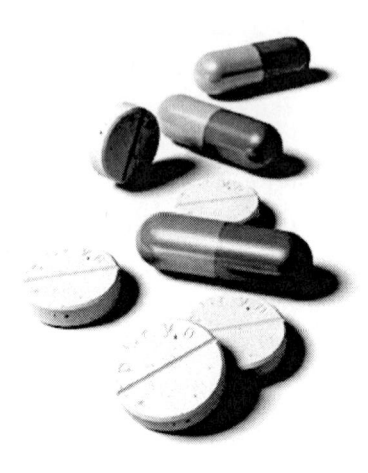

The above drugs are stimulants (or uppers).

They will give you a feeling known as a rush, and can bring on a feeling of euphoria (excitement).

However, what goes up must come down!

All of the above drugs (remember that alcohol is a drug too) work by stimulating the happy chemicals in your brain (dopamine).

Imagine these happy chemicals are like muscles; if you run a race and work your muscles really hard then you will go really fast, which is great, but afterwards your muscles will be tired, and even quite wobbly. They probably won't work well for a while.

This is the same with our happy chemicals - we overwork them when we are 'high' on the drug, then once the drug has worn off, we have less happy chemicals to use. The receptor (that allows these happy chemicals to work) gets tired. It has been overworked. What happens when we are tired? We go to sleep – so do our happy chemical receptors.

So are sleepy happy chemical receptors going to work properly? No they are not. Leading to…

You've guessed it, **depression!**

Anabolic Steroids and Diet Pills

We all want great bodies, and if we can find a way of burning fat and creating great muscles without putting in the hard work shouldn't we take that route?

The simple answer is **NO!**

Anabolic Steroids are drugs (either injected or in tablet form) that enhance muscles. They will give you the biceps of 'The Terminator", however unfortunately, they will also give his temper.

Anabolic steroids, as well as many illegal diet pills can cause the worst rage imaginable, put pressure on your heart and leave you feeling depressed and anxious.

Steroids are banned in body-building and athletic competitions because of their horrendous side effects and I advise you or anyone you know to most definitely stay away from them.

Many illegal diet pills can be bought on the internet and in so called 'diet clinics' however, most, if not all of these will contain amphetamine (speed).

Unfortunately, the only way to burn fat and build muscle is by doing the good old fashioned tried and tested method of eating healthily (more protein to build muscle) and taking more exercise. On the plus side, exercise boosts your happy chemicals naturally, therefore making you feel **GREAT!**

The 'Come Down'

As I said before, 'what goes up must come down'. One minute we are dancing away having the time of our lives. Then when the drug wears off we suffer what is called a 'come-down'.

The effects of this are tiredness, sadness, confusion, paranoia and even suicidal thoughts.

Is the 'high' really worth it?

Ok so the come-down won't last that long right?

WRONG!

A typical come-down can last most of the following day, or even the next few days. However, sometimes it can last a lifetime.

Imagine that! Being stuck in a come-down forever.

Just like cannabis, these drugs can trigger mental health problems that can affect the rest of the person's life.

So let's look at this scenario...

8pm

You're at a house party with friends; someone offers you a little pill or some white powder and tells you it will give you "The time of your life". You don't want to appear uncool, and you're excited about experiencing that great buzz that everyone is talking about. So you say yes.

It feels ok....a bit worrying to start with as your heart starts to beat faster. Your head swims a little and you feel slightly confused. But then you start having fun, you feel happy and confident.

11pm

Starting to feel a bit sick, headache is starting. You could go home to bed? Or you could take some more?

Whatever you decide to do, you'll still have to suffer the effects of a hideous 'come down'. Although, if you take more, obviously the 'come down' will be a lot worse.

12am

Paranoia begins!

You don't want to look at anyone, you feel as though everyone is staring at you. 'Why are they looking at me?'

'Are they talking about me?'

'Why do I feel like this?'

You start to shake, and your stomach hurts now. It's rumbling and feels as though….. Oh no, not right here in front of everyone, now that would be so embarrassing. Please NO! …

Too late!

Time to leave!

You were due home at 11, 'uh-oh, you're in trouble'

You go home, can hardly look your parents in the eye. You feel paranoid. 'They know. Surely they do'

You go to bed. But can't sleep…

Here come those paranoid thoughts again…

'Everyone hates me'

You start to cry. Then can't stop.

'Why do I feel so low?'

You're shaking. Head doesn't feel right. Feel confused. Heart beating faster again. Feel sick.

4am

Finally, you sleep. Only, you have a head full of nightmares, not dreams.

10am

You wake up. Your mouth feels dry. You feel sick, and your head is so confused.

You pull the covers back over your head. Can't face going downstairs. Don't want to see anyone. Can't speak.

'Why do I feel so low?'

You start to cry again. And can't stop again.

'Why did I take that stuff? I feel rubbish, it wasn't worth it. I can't wait for tomorrow to come, I'll be okay tomorrow'

OR WILL YOU?

If you're unlucky your 'come down' could last and last and last.

There are many people, I know personally, whose future has been decided by an awful depression caused by taking drugs when they were younger.

Even when you stop, the depression can still last.

Think of it like this… if you abuse your body it won't work properly. It's the same with your brain. Look after your brain; you only have one of them. If you burn out your happy chemicals, then how will you be happy?

Remember What goes up must come down*!*

Case study *(names have been changed to protect identities)*

Lucy * aged 27

Lucy was a fun loving, popular teenager. At 16 she enjoyed partying, and when she realised that her crowd was taking E's, speed and cocaine she decided that of course she would too.

They would go out on weekends and look forward to buzzing, dance to their hearts content all night long without getting tired, and feeling more confident than ever.

She felt great so how these drugs possibly be bad? The come-down's weren't too bad. Her friends suffered them far worse than she did. Luckily she wasn't too affected by them like some people were. Life was fun!

A few months in, Lucy noticed that the come-downs did start to affect her, then they became really bad, every weekend they were getting worse. They would last longer, and the sadness wasn't just sadness anymore. It was turning into despair. Sometimes on a Sunday she would sit and cry all day. She would feel paranoid, and sure that no one actually liked her.

Slowly Lucy realised that she was turning into the opposite of herself.

This fun loving, confident teenager was beginning to feel upset over the slightest thing, paranoid, and even started to suffer panic attacks.

She decided to stop. When her friends were handing out the drugs she would pretend to take them, but go into the toilets and flush them away. After all she didn't want to 'appear odd'.

She still had a fantastic time, danced all night, and laughed just as much as she had before.

The come-downs stopped and life was great again….

For a few years anyway…

Several years' later depression set in. It didn't make sense to her. She was happy. Life was great. What was going on?

Lucy went to the doctor. She explained her symptoms, and her doctor asked her about her lifestyle. She told him the truth; she didn't drink much alcohol, ate a healthy diet, took exercise and had no stressful situations at present.

Then the doctor asked about her past. He told her that her symptoms were typical of someone who's 'happy chemical receptors' were not working as they should.

She told him about her brush with drugs. She explained that it was recreational (only on weekends) and only lasted for a short period of her life.

To cut a long story short, her happy chemicals were depleted (run out). In a manner of speaking she had worn them out.

How had that tiny part of her life affected her so many years on?

Why had it happened to her, when other people could get away with no symptoms what so ever?

But had they?...

Over the next few years, as Lucy was slowly getting better through the help of the right medication, counselling and support, she found out that the crowd that she used to party with were all suffering in their own way.

Many had suffered such terrible panic attacks; they couldn't even leave their houses.

Another had committed suicide (this a true story remember).

A couple of them had spent time in a mental institution, two had suffered terrifying hallucinations (seeing things that aren't actually there), and one had become an alcoholic - and the last Lucy heard, was awaiting a liver transplant, if he doesn't get one soon he will probably die.

Lucy's advice – *"Even though it is fun at the time, you don't know what the future consequences will be. When you are young it is hard to imagine being an adult, you just want to live for today, but you **do** get older, and do you really want your future to be one full of mental illness, or physical problems? Don't ruin your life with drugs or too much alcohol. I wish I'd listened when people said the same to me. My future would be so different"*

~~~~~~~~~~~~~~~~~~~~~~~~~~~~

I have many case studies such as the one above. They are real people, either that I know personally, or that I met when doing drug studies whilst undertaking my Psychology courses. In fact, the names have been changed to protect identities, how do you know one of them isn't, in fact, me?

The statistics speak for themselves. If, in a large group of people who took drugs recreationally (just occasionally), none of them appeared not to be affected by future side effects, doesn't that tell us something?

In other words, the majority of people who take drugs will have their mental health affected in some way, either during, or in the future.

Is the 'high' worth it? The evidence above states not!

Just say NO!

Is it easy to say "NO?"

Not always. It's quite tricky if everyone else is doing it.

If you have the confidence to say no then well done, that's fantastic.

I know that now I would most definitely say no. However, I remember that when I was your age it was harder. It would be embarrassing. I would be seen as the 'social weirdo' wouldn't i?

I hope that you will find the confidence to say NO if you ever get offered any 'stuff' (remember what I said in chapter 1 – most friends would be glad that you stuck your hand up and said NO, because maybe they are feeling the same).

But if you don't, then why not do as Lucy did? Throw them away. It isn't the most honest way of getting out of taking drugs, but it is better than taking them.

The best, most positive way to get away from that scene altogether is to get new friends. Easier said than done? Well, do it a step at a time. Step back from the pushy ones, make yourself less available by pretending you are busy, and don't answer the phone to them as much as usual. Hang out at different places where you can meet new people.

Why?

Because your future is yours and yours alone! They may not be there when you are going through your depression, panic attacks and phobias. Of course they won't be – they will be too busy going through their own; or worse!

As I said before, you only have one brain. It may sound boring, and not much fun at all. But please look after it.

Lack of sleep

We need sleep. This much is obvious. As I stated in the insomnia part of the book, without sleep we can become grumpy, snappy and unmotivated. Our brain feels fuzzy and doesn't seem to work properly.

We can also become really depressed. It may be tempting to stay up playing games consoles, or watching television, or hanging out with our mates, but the effects can be awful if we do it too much.

Next time you stay up extra late, note your mood the next morning. Do you feel happy, alive and full of energy?

Or do you feel tired, flat and quite down in the dumps?

It is a proven fact that you teenagers actually need more sleep than you did when you were younger, in order to function properly. Your body is going through massive hormonal changes. It needs enough sleep time to re-fuel.

Sleep may seem boring, but it re-charges us, Just like your mobile telephone we need charging too. So, if you want to feel great every day, make sure you get enough sleep.

Diet

Food is our fuel. If we are filling our body with the wrong fuel it won't work properly.

We wouldn't put any old rubbish into our car to make it work. We use the best fuel. So let's do the same with ourselves.

Sugar causes tiredness. Tiredness can cause depressive feelings.

Don't get me wrong I LOVE sugar! Sugar is the best, most tasty, gorgeous substance that has ever come into my life. If I could, I would bathe in the stuff. I ADORE it!

But….

It doesn't adore me.

After the energy rush that sugar gives us, we slump.

You know the motto by now…come on, altogether…

 "What goes up must come down"

Next time you have a lovely cake, or chocolate bar, pay attention to how you feel an hour or so later. We get what is called a 'sugar crash' or 'carb crash'.

So if you are eating a lot of sugar throughout the day then you are crashing, and slumping constantly. This leaves you exhausted, and your brain too tired to concentrate on anything at all.

The same happens with 'stodgy' food. So if you nip off to the chip shop for lunch a few times a week, now, maybe you can understand why you are so tired in the afternoons.

Our bodies need vitamins and minerals. In other words we need a little visit from Mr Fruit and Mrs Vegetable from time to time. Preferably 5 times a day.

Fatty, stodgy food and sugar is okay in moderation, but if we are having it in our daily diet then our insides won't really thank us for it.

Even if it does not affect our weight it can affect our organs, and, just as importantly, our mood.

Another weapon on the fight to banish tiredness, and therefore lift your mood, is to drink enough fluids every day. Many of us don't.

Our bodies need a certain amount of fluid to function properly. Try this simple exercise…

Next time you are feeling tired have a large drink of water, and watch your energy levels rise. The same works on headaches, water helps them disappear. Try it. I promise it works!

There are certain foods that include chemical mood lifters. These are lettuce, turkey and bananas to name a few. Any foods or supplements containing Zinc will help your mood, as will B vitamins.

It is also important to remember to eat enough, and regularly.

If you are denying yourself food then you are denying your brain the fuel that it needs. You can watch your weight and still eat enough. Watch **what** you eat, rather than the **amount** that you eat.

You know that your body and mind will suffer if you starve it. So be kind to it, and yourself by giving yourself the fuel to help your body and brain survive.

So, to summarise; allow yourself a little of what you fancy, but ensure that you are getting some of the good stuff also.

Eat regularly, and drink plenty of healthy fluids. Following these tips will not only keep you looking gorgeous, but also help your mood as your blood sugar levels will be stable. The happy chemicals in your brain will thank you for it.

Chapter.7. Mood Lifters – or how to get

HAPPY!

Okay, so we've talked about what we shouldn't do in order to stay happy, now let's talk about what we should do. Here follows a simple list of tried and tested mood lifters...

- **Getting creative** - drawing/writing poetry or stories, can all really help you express yourself, and take your mind off your troubles too

- **Pamper yourself** – no matter if you are a girl or a boy, everyone loves a bit of pampering. Run yourself a lovely warm bubble bath, soak in it and relax.

- **Music** – listening to music is a sure fire way to make you feel great. Pay attention to how different music makes you feel. Then choose something that makes you feel happy. Even compile a list of mood- lifting music then put it on whenever you want a boost.

- **Rest** – sleep always helps our moods.

- **Exercise** – helpful hormones called *endorphins* are released into our system when we exercise. They make us feel happy naturally.

- **Treat time** – Be kind to yourself. Reward yourself when you feel you deserve it. (Which should be a lot). It doesn't have to cost money. A treat could even be watching your favourite show.

- **Comedy** – laughing really is the best medicine. Watch a comedy DVD. Meet with friends that you know always make you laugh. Or simply pull funny faces at yourself in the mirror. Speak in a funny voice, and make yourself laugh. Be nuts, act crazy, no one can see you. And 'so what' if they can!

- **Smile** – Honestly, it works. Smiling creates that old favourite…that's right, those happy hormones!

<u>*Try at home task:*</u> *Make a list of what make you happy. Spend time thinking about what makes you smile. Then make sure that you do something from your list every week.*

Chapter. 8. The Life plan – or how to get direction

Being a teenager is a difficult time. "Am I an adult?" "Am I still a child?"

It is hard to know who you are and where you are going. So this is where the life plan should help....

This life plan will help you to think about what you wish to do when you are older, where you want to be, and how to get there. You don't want to simply end up in a job that you are not happy with do you? You want financial stability don't you? Then start your journey to health, wealth and happiness today.

Answer the following questions, either in this book, or on a separate piece of paper...

1. **What do you enjoy doing? List your hobbies here...**

2. **Would you like your future career to include your hobbies (things that you enjoy doing)?**

   (For example if you like to draw, think about how you could incorporate this into your job) Write a list of your hobbies here...

3. Write a list of jobs that include your hobbies here…

   (For example if you like art and computers write down 'graphic designer'

   If you enjoy sports or swimming write down 'lifeguard' or 'sports teacher')

4. Now think about the qualifications you need for that job (You can find this out by typing it into the Internet. Simply Google 'what qualifications do I need to be a….?' Or ask your career advisor at school)

It is really exciting to have something to work towards. If you know which qualifications you will need, then you can start working towards getting them. Look up information on your local colleges and universities. Ask in your local career office, or job centre, and look forward to your future. You CAN do it you know, why not!

Chapter. 9. Bullying – or, how to beat it, be assertive, and get your groove back!

Being bullied is not usually about the bully hating you. Believe it or not, it is normally about the bully hating themselves.

People who bully are often feeling insecure about themselves. This can sometimes result in a person throwing their weight around to make themselves feel more important.

When a bully has low self esteem, they often feel they need approval from others. They want to gain respect from their peers. The quickest way to get respect 'they think' is to create fear in others.

Many think that if they are feared, then others will think of them as 'mighty' and 'powerful'. *"Oh here comes Billy bully, he's so strong. I would never mess with him. What a power he has!"*

In actual fact I can guarantee his classmates are thinking *"Oh here comes Billy bully throwing his weight around again, trying to make himself look important. What an idiot!"*

Studies have shown that the class bullies are often being bullied themselves, probably at home. Not all, but many bullies become that way because of unhappiness at home, and therefore want to take some control back into their lives by doing the same to others. It is wrong, and doesn't make much sense, but it is a fact, in a lot of cases.

Well, I know this doesn't change your opinion of the bully. I know they are still being a 'tool', and it is no excuse for their behaviour. BUT, maybe it will help you to realise that if you are being bullied, it is never because you deserve it, or because you are a 'drip' or a 'nerd'. It is often because they can see you as an easy target if you are not the kind of person that normally stands up for yourself. So it would be a great idea to learn how to be bully proof!

Assertiveness

The word assertive means: to stand up for yourself without being aggressive.

Aggression – To be aggressive means to make people feel afraid by shouting, punching or swearing.

Passive - To be passive means that you are allowing people to do and say whatever they want to you regardless of how it makes you feel.

Neither of these are a great choice. Being aggressive will ensure people are afraid of you (thus turning you into a bully) and won't make you very popular, whereas being passive is a terrible idea also. Passive people often get bossed around, bullied and often lose respect from their friends.

It is perfect to become something between the two. This is called assertiveness…

Now, first let's take a look at your rights a human being…

- the right to be treated with respect
- the right to make mistakes and not be laughed at
- the right to refuse requests without having to feel guilty
- the right to ask for what you want (realising that the other person has the right to say 'no')
- the right to be listened to and to be taken seriously
- the right to say "I don't understand"
- The right to say *"I don't like how you are treating me"*

Now if someone is not treating you with respect and repeatedly hurting your feelings then they are bullying you. Even our friends can bully us sometimes.

So we need to learn how to say *"I don't like how you are treating me, please stop"*

Sometimes we need to get even tougher and take out the please…*"I really don't like how you are treating me, STOP NOW"*

You have every right to tell someone if they are hurting your feelings.

Take a deep breath; look them straight in the eye (this is more difficult than it sounds, but it shows that you mean what you say, so it's worth doing). Now state your point, tell them how you are feeling (practise it beforehand if you like).

Their reaction? They may laugh. If this is the case. Tell them that you had expected that. This will shock them, and help them to see that you are behaving like an adult. You will actually have the upper hand.

Say NO if you want to!

WE can often get bullied into doing things we really don't want to do. If people pressure us enough, us human beings can crack.

An example of this can be when it comes to drugs, smoking, or sex. If someone nags us to do one of the above we can feel pressured to do it, just because their behaviour is making us feel awkward. Sometimes it's just easier to say yes right? **Wrong!**

Think about YOUR feelings. Do you really want to do the thing that you are getting nagged into doing? It doesn't matter if your friends are doing it. Do YOU want to do it?

If the answer is no, then don't do it. Say no.

I know it's easier said than done. Maybe you will get laughed at, but if you do, it will only be for a moment. Then that moment will pass and you will be left with your dignity intact (as well as your health). It's all too easy to say yes to something, only to regret it later and wish that you had stuck to your guns and said a big fat **NO** (especially when you are left with a drug or smoking induced illness, a sexually transmitted infection, or are left holding the baby, literally!)

Body language

Assertiveness isn't just about what we say, but our actions also. In other words, how we carry ourselves.

Act confident, even if you don't feel it. Use your body to help you look confident. Confident people are less likely to be bullied or attacked.

When I was your age I learned about something called NVC (non verbal communication) and it helped me carry myself with confidence. Try this…

Stand tall, do not slump. Shoulders down and back, and head held high.

Practise it now, go on…

How do you feel? More confident?

How do you look? Look in the mirror.

Now keep looking in the mirror and slump your shoulders and drop your head. How do you look now?

Which **you** looks best? Which one would win an argument, or look as though they could stand up for themselves?

If you **act** assertive, then you **feel** more assertive!

So stand tall again, stand up straight, shoulders back, head up and look like a somebody, not a nobody. Change the way you carry yourself. Even if you don't feel assertive, act as though you do.

Hold up that fantastic head of yours, and smile. You have every right to be here on this planet. Show the bullies who the boss of you is ... # YOU!

Bullying Case Studies

Below are some real life stories from people who were bullied, they share their experiences and give their advice to you, or anyone you know that needs it.

Rueben age 13.

"It was hard at break-times, because I would try to fit in, but I felt like the odd one out because they wouldn't let me join in. I felt as though I was pushed out of the group.

It was a group of boys; they didn't call me names or anything, but wouldn't let me in their crowd, and would laugh at me.

There was no one to play with.

Then I started to get hurt by one boy. He would strangle me, and pushed me in the throat.

After a while i told my Mum and she spoke to the headmaster, and also to the boy's Mother. It stopped after that. I'm glad I told my Mum.

This all happened when I was in primary school. Now I am in Comprehensive school, and I am so much happier. I have lots of friends, and have a laugh at school every day. I look forward to school now instead of dreading it".

Rueben's advice – *"Tell someone straight away, don't keep it to yourself. Grown-ups can help you out, but that's not the only way; if you find it tricky with adults you could even tell your friends, or after lesson in school take a teacher to the side and explain and tell them you've had enough. There are many ways to deal with this situation. If it happened to me now I would definitely tell someone and stop the bullies. They may think it's cool to pick on someone and hurt people's feelings but people watching from a distance who the bullies are trying to impress just think the bullies are total jerks, I would never put up with it if it happened again."*

Case Study 2

Carrie's story

"I was bullied from the age of 14 and it lasted till i was 16.

It only ended because the head teacher caught me out of lesson when i shouldn't have been. By then it felt it was too late, the damage had been done I was at school leaving age, and I had spent the last two years hating school.

Carrie's advice: *"*

I should of changed schools really, or told the head teacher when it had first begun. My advice would be to always tell someone. Don't suffer alone.

Useful Links

BULLYING ADVICE

Kidscape

5 star anti cyber bullying site featuring great advice for students, parents and teachers

www.kidscape.org.uk

Childline

A fantastic site which offers help and advice on just about everything you can think of, not just bullying.

www.childline.org.uk/Bullying

DRUG AND ALCOHOL MISUSE

Drugline

They can provide support, help and information, not only to sufferers, but also to their parents, grandparents, carers, partners and children of those with drug and alcohol problems. Anyone affected by drugs or alcohol misuse is welcome.

Freephone Crisis & Support Line: 0808 1 606 606

Email support: help@drugsline.org

www.drugsline.org

Talk to Frank

An excellent, easy to understand website packed full of advice, stories, info and with a brilliant FREE helpline too. You can even text your drugs question - you don't have to use your real name - and FRANK will get back to you:

Text: 82111 (The cost of sending a text to FRANK is the same as a standard text message - which will depend on your network tariff.)

Email: (type this into your address bar)
http://www.talktofrank.com/form.aspx?id=3665

Telephone: 0800 77 66 00 www.talktofrank.com

SELF HARM HELP

CALM – campaign against living miserably

"If you're feeling like you want to hurt yourself, and want some help, give CALM a call and talk about the way you feel. We won't judge you in any way – we'll just try and help you find another way to cope with your worries"

Telephone: 0800 58 58 58 (FREE)

HELP WITH EATING DISORDERS

CALM – campaign against living miserably

A fabulous FREE suicide prevention helpline (which will not show up on your phone bill) and online support system ie: forums and helpful real articles. Although CALM is targeted at young men aged between 15-35, they actually offer help, information and support via a helpline and website to anyone calling within the UK, regardless of age, gender or geographic location.

www.thecalmzone.net

Telephone: 0800 58 58 58

Anorexia and Bulimia Care

Supports sufferers and their carers of anorexia, bulimia and compulsive eating disorders.

Telephone: 01934 710645

www.anorexiabulimiacare.co.uk

Beat

Charity offering help, advice and support for anyone whose life is affected by eating disorders.

Telephone: 0845 634 1414

www.b-eat.co.uk

Men Get Eating Disorders Too

A new website site for men who have been affected by anorexia, bulimia, binge eating disorder, compulsive eating and/or exercise and bigorexia. The main aim of the site is to raise awareness of eating disorders in men to enable men to seek support.

www.mengetedstoo.co.uk

Debbie Wildi is presently taking Teen Relax workshops into School classrooms and youth centres in the UK, and more recently offering INSET days to enable teachers to train in the various Teen Relax techniques to help their pupils overcome stress symptoms.

For more information on Teen Relax teacher training, workshops and seminars contact Debbie

debbie@truerelax.co.uk

Or see www.truerelax.co.uk

Teen Relax is a part of the True Relax Company. All techniques, logo's and branding are copyrighted and protected by the proprietor of True Relax.